IN THE BEGINNING
The Seven Days of Creation

editor and publisher
Maryjane Hooper Tonn

In the beginning God created the heaven and the earth. And the earth was without form, and void; and darkness was upon the face of the deep. And the Spirit of God moved upon the face of the waters.

Genesis 1:1-2

Inspiring thoughts on the beauty of God's Creation.

And God said, Let there be light: and there was light. And God saw the light, that it was good: and God divided the light from the darkness. And God called the light Day, and the darkness he called Night. And the evening and the morning were the first day.

Genesis 1:3-5

IDEALS PUBLISHING CORP., MILWAUKEE, WIS. 53201
© COPYRIGHT MCMLXXVII, PRINTED AND BOUND IN U.S.A.

Give me the splendid sun
with all his beams full-dazzling . . .
Walt Whitman

This is the day which the Lord hath made;
we will rejoice and be glad in it.
Psalm 118:24

It is necessary for me to see the first point of light which begins to be dawn. It is necessary to be present alone at the resurrection of Day, in the blank silence when the sun appears. In this completely neutral instant I receive from the Eastern woods, the tall oaks, the one word "Day," which is never the same. It is never spoken in any known language.

Thomas Merton

Mysterious Night! when our first parent knew
Thee from report divine, and heard thy name,
Did he not tremble for this lovely frame,
This glorious canopy of light and blue?
Yet 'neath a curtain of translucent dew,
Bathed in the rays of the great setting flame,
Hesperus with the host of heaven came,
And lo! Creation widened in man's view.

Joseph Blanco White

To me every hour of the light
and dark is a miracle.
Every cubic inch of space
is a miracle.

Walt Whitman

And God said, Let there be a firmament in the midst of the waters, and let it divide the waters from the waters. And God made the firmament, and divided the waters which were under the firmament from the waters which were above the firmament: and it was so. And God called the firmament Heaven. And the evening and the morning were the second day.

Genesis 1:6-8

Look unto the heavens, and see;
and behold the clouds
which are higher than thou.

Job 35:5

The man who can really, in living union of the mind and heart, converse with God through nature finds in the material forms around him a source of power and happiness inexhaustible and like the life of angels. The highest life and glory of man is to be alive unto God; and when this grandeur of sensibility to him and this power of communication with him is carried as the habit of the soul into the forms of nature, then the walls of our world are as the gates of heaven.

George B. Cheever

The blue of heaven is larger than the clouds.

Elizabeth Barrett Browning

I will give unto thee the keys
of the kingdom of heaven . . .

Matthew 16:19

I never saw a moor,
I never saw the sea;
Yet know I how the heather looks,
And what a wave must be.

I never spoke with God,
Nor visited in heaven;
Yet certain am I of the spot
As if the chart were given.

Emily Dickinson

The way to Heaven out of all places
is of like length and distance.

Thomas More

And God said, Let the waters under the heaven be gathered together unto one place, and let the dry land appear: and it was so. And God called the dry land Earth; and the gathering together of the waters called he Seas: and God saw that it was good. And God said, Let the earth bring forth grass, the herb yielding seed, and the fruit tree yielding fruit after his kind, whose seed is in itself, upon the earth: and it was so. And the earth brought forth grass, and herb yielding seed after his kind, and the tree yielding fruit, whose seed was in itself, after his kind: and God saw that it was good. And the evening and the morning were the third day.

Genesis 1:9-13

O Lord, how manifold are thy works!
in wisdom hast thou made them all:
the earth is full of thy riches.

Psalm 104:24

The sea hath no king but God alone.

D. G. Rossetti

There is a pleasure in the pathless woods,
There is a rapture on the lonely shore;
There is society, where none intrudes,
By the deep sea, and music in its roar.

Lord Byron

Driftwood

Driftwood marks the shore—
The alphabet of ancients
Writing a last word.

Daniel Smythe

From GREEN DOORS by Daniel Smythe, published by The Golden Quill Press.

Climb the mountains and get their good tidings.
The winds will blow their own freshness into you,
And the storms their energy, while cares will
Drop away from you like the leaves of Autumn.

John Muir

I will lift up mine eyes unto the hills,
from whence cometh my help. My help cometh
from the Lord, which made heaven and earth.

Psalm 121:1-2

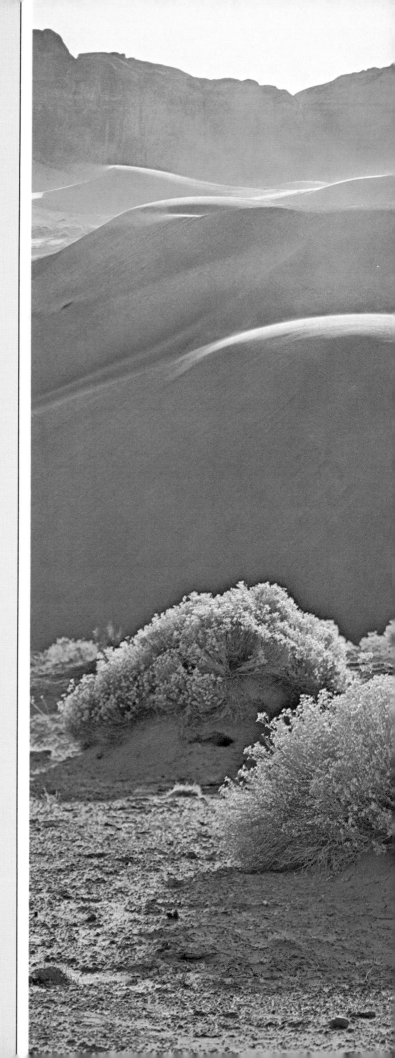

The wilderness
and the solitary place
shall be glad for them;
and the desert shall
rejoice, and blossom
as the rose.

Isaiah 35:1

The groves were God's first temples. Ere man learned to hew the shaft, and lay the architrave, and spread the roof above them— ere he framed the lofty vault, to gather and roll back the sound of anthems; in the darkling wood, amidst the cool and silence, he knelt down and offered to the Mightiest solemn thanks and supplication.

William Cullen Bryant

Treetops . . .
Voices of the
Melodious winds, hum
Tunes that fortify
faith in things
Not seen.

Beatrice Branch

. . . The rain
falls upon the earth
and grass and flowers
come
      perfectly
into form from its
              liquid
clearness . . .

William Carlos Williams

A child said, What is grass? fetching it to me with full
    hands;
How could I answer the child? . . . I do not know what it
    is any more than he.

I guess it must be the flag of my disposition, out of hopeful
    green stuff woven.

Or I guess it is the handkerchief of the Lord,
A scented gift and remembrancer designedly dropped,
Bearing the owner's name someway in the corners, that we
    may see and remark, and say Whose?

Or I guess the grass is itself a child . . . the produced babe
    of the vegetation.

Walt Whitman

Never lose an opportunity of seeing anything that is beautiful; for beauty is God's handwriting– a wayside sacrament. Welcome it in every fair face, in every fair sky, in every fair flower, and thank God for it as a cup of blessing.

Ralph Waldo Emerson

To the Daisy

With little here to do or see
Of things that in the great world be,
Sweet Daisy! oft I talk to thee
    For thou art worthy,
Thou unassuming commonplace
Of Nature, with that homely face,
And yet with something of a grace
    Which love makes for thee!

Sweet Flower! for by that name at last
When all my reveries are past,
I call thee, and to that cleave fast,
    Sweet silent Creature!
That breath'st with me in sun and air,
Do thou, as thou art wont, repair
My heart with gladness, and a share
    Of thy meek nature!

William Wordsworth

His tenderness in the springing grass,
His beauty in the flowers,
His living love in the sun above—
All here, and near, and ours!

Samuel Gilman

The mountains are God's thoughts piled up.
The ocean is God's thoughts spread out.
The flowers are God's thoughts in bloom.
The dewdrops are God's thoughts in pearls.

Samuel Jones

Green River

When breezes are soft and skies are fair,
I steal an hour from study and care,
And hie me away to the woodland scene,
Where wanders the stream with waters of green,
As if the bright fringe of herbs on its brink
Had given their stain to the waves they drink;
And they, whose meadows it murmurs through,
Have named the stream from its own fair hue.

William Cullen Bryant

I do set my bow in the cloud, and it shall be for
a token of a covenant between me and the earth.

Genesis 9:13

Walk on a rainbow trail,
Walk on a trail of song,
And all about you will be beauty.
There is a way
Out of every dark mist,
Over a rainbow trail.

Navajo Song

And God said, Let there be lights in the firmament of the heaven to divide the day from the night; and let them be for signs, and for seasons, and for days, and years: And let them be for lights in the firmament of the heaven to give light upon the earth: and it was so. And God made two great lights; the greater light to rule the day, and the lesser light to rule the night: he made the stars also. And God set them in the firmament of the heaven to give light upon the earth, And to rule over the day and over the night, and to divide the light from the darkness: and God saw that it was good. And the evening and the morning were the fourth day.

Genesis 1:14-19

One sun by day; by night ten thousand shine, and light us deep into the deity. How boundless in magnificence and might! Stars teach us as well as shine, and every student of the night inspire; the elder scripture writ by God's own hand, authentic, uncorrupt by man.

Edward Young

A star is beautiful; it affords pleasure, not from what it is to do, or to give, but simply by being what it is. It benefits the heavens; it has congruity with the mighty space in which it dwells. It has repose; no force disturbs its eternal peace. It has freedom; no obstruction lies between it and infinity.

Thomas Carlyle

Silently one by one,
In the infinite meadows of heaven,
Blossomed the lovely stars,
The forget-me-nots of the angels.
Henry Wadsworth Longfellow

The seasons come and go,
and go and come,
to teach men gratitude.

Robert Pollok

While the earth remaineth, seedtime and harvest,
and cold and heat, and summer and winter,
and day and night shall not cease.

Genesis 8:22

And God said, Let the waters bring forth abundantly the moving creature that hath life, and fowl that may fly above the earth in the open firmament of heaven. And God created great whales, and every living creature that moveth, which the waters brought forth abundantly, after their kind, and every winged fowl after his kind: and God saw that it was good. And God blessed them, saying, Be fruitful, and multiply, and fill the waters in the seas, and let fowl multiply in the earth. And the evening and the morning were the fifth day.

Genesis 1:20-23

Speak to the earth, and it shall teach thee;
and the fishes of the sea shall declare unto thee.

Job 12:8

If you were to make little fishes talk,
They would talk like whales.

Oliver Goldsmith

To have faith is to have wings.

Sir James M. Barrie

Behold the fowls of the air: for they sow not,
neither do they reap, nor gather into barns; yet
your heavenly Father feedeth them. Are ye not
much better than they?

Matthew 6:26

What are wings but flesh and bone
And flashing feathers? These alone
Bear the blue jay, wild and free,
From low earth to hilltop tree.
These alone lift hawk and wren
To a world beyond the ken
Of the lizard and the hare
Or the panther in his lair.
What are wings? They are to me
Soundless song and poetry
Etched, wherever wild birds fly,
On the fresh page of the sky.

S. Omar Barker

And God said, Let the earth bring forth the living creature after his kind, cattle, and creeping thing, and beast of the earth after his kind: and it was so. And God made the beast of the earth after his kind, and cattle after their kind, and every thing that creepeth upon the earth after his kind: and God saw that it was good. And God said, Let us make man in our image, after our likeness: and let them have dominion over the fish of the sea, and over the fowl of the air, and over the cattle, and over all the earth, and over every creeping thing that creepeth upon the earth. So God created man in his own image, in the image of God created he him; male and female created he them. And God blessed them, and God said unto them, Be fruitful, and multiply, and replenish the earth, and subdue it: and have dominion over the fish of the sea, and over the fowl of the air, and over every living thing that moveth upon the earth. And God said, Behold, I have given you every herb bearing seed, which is upon the face of all the earth, and every tree, in the which is the fruit of a tree yielding seed; to you it shall be for meat. And to every beast of the earth, and to every fowl of the air, and to every thing that creepeth upon the earth, wherein there is life, I have given every green herb for meat: and it was so. And God saw every thing that he had made, and, behold, it was very good. And the evening and the morning were the sixth day.

Genesis 1:24-31

And the Lord God formed man of the dust of the ground, and breathed into his nostrils the breath of life; and man became a living soul.

Genesis 2:7

Nothing in life is to be feared;
It is only to be understood.

Marie Curie

We ought not childishly neglect the study of the meaner animals, because there is something wonderful in all nature . . . We ought to investigate all sorts of animals, because all of them will reveal something of nature and something of beauty.

Aristotle

Almost any man may, like the spider,
spin from his own inwards his own citadel.

John Keats

Why does the spider make her web tighter in one place and slacker in another? Why now make one sort of knot and then another, if she has not deliberation, thought and conclusion? We sufficiently discover in most of their works how much animals excel us, and how weak our art is to imitate them. We see, nevertheless, in our ruder performances that we there employ all our faculties, and apply the utmost power of our souls; why do we not conclude the same of thee?

Michel de Montaigne

The commonest things of nature have qualities
    and characteristics which are stupendous.
They are a revelation to the persons
    who study and analyze them.
Most people, however, find only strange
    and unusual things worth wondering about,
While they take ordinary things for granted.

Saint Augustine

He prayeth well who loveth well
Both man and bird and beast . . .

He prayeth best who loveth best
All things both great and small;

For the dear God who loveth us,
He made and loveth all.

Samuel Coleridge

Blue-Butterfly Day

It is blue-butterfly day here in spring,
And with these sky-flakes down in flurry on flurry
There is more unmixed color on the wing
Than flowers will show for days unless they hurry.

But these are flowers that fly and all but sing:
And now from having ridden out desire
They lie closed over in the wind and cling
Where wheels have freshly sliced the April mire.

Robert Frost

One touch of nature
makes the whole world kin.

William Shakespeare

God can be known chiefly through
His works, and animate nature
is the most wonderful of these works.

John Ray

I think I could turn and live with the animals,
they are so placid and self-contain'd,
I stand and look at them long and long.

Walt Whitman

Thus the heavens and the earth were finished, and all the host of them. And on the seventh day God ended his work which he had made; and he rested on the seventh day from all his work which he had made.

Genesis 2:1-2

designed by
Robin Lee Dennison

Managing Editor, Ralph Luedtke
Associate Editor, Julie Hogan
Photographic Editor, Gerald Koser
Production Editor, Stuart L. Zyduck